2019 - 2020

Dates	Signature Required (Priest or Deacon)
Oct. 19/20	
Oct. 26/27	
Nov. 2/3	
Nov. 9/10	
Nov. 16/17	
Nov. 23/24	
Nov.30/Dec. 1	
Dec. 7/8	
Dec. 14/15	
Dec. 21/22	
Christmas Day	
Dec. 28/29	
Jan. 1	
Jan. 4/5	
Jan. 11/12	
Jan. 18/19	
Jan. 25/26	
Feb. 1/2	
Feb. 8/9	
Feb. 15/16	
Feb. 22/23	
Feb, 29/Mar.1	
Mar. 7/8	
Mar. 14/15	
Mar. 21/22	
Mar. 28/29	
Apr. 4/5	
Apr. 11/12	
April 18/19	
April 25/26	
May 2/3	

Nihil Obstat
✠ Most Reverend Robert C. Morlino

Imprimatur
✠ Most Reverend Robert C. Morlino
Bishop of Madison
December 28, 2004

The *Nihil Obstat* and *Imprimatur* are official declarations
that a book or pamphlet is free of doctrinal or moral error.
No implication is contained therein that those who have
granted the *Nihil Obstat* and *Imprimatur* agree with the
contents, opinions, or statements expressed.

Printed in the United States of America.

𝕊 is a registered trademark of William H. Sadlier, Inc.

William H. Sadlier, Inc.
9 Pine Street
New York, NY 10005-4700

ISBN: 978-0-8215-5728-0
10 11 12 13 14 15 WEBC 22 21 20 19 18

My Mass Book

CONTENTS

The Mass

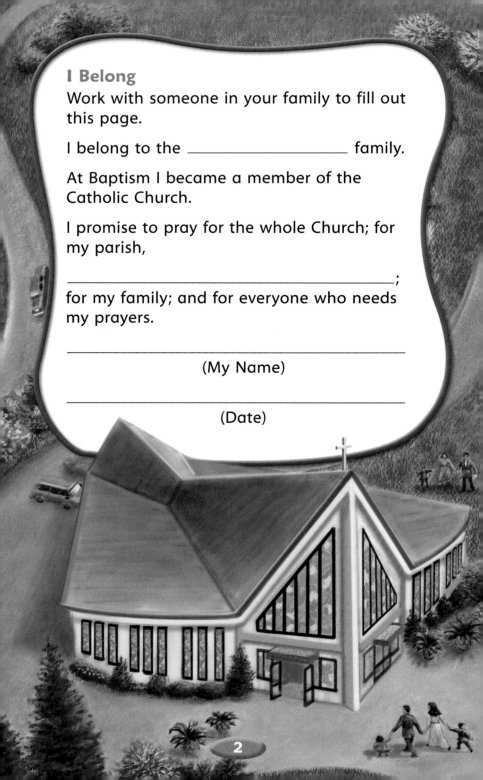

I Belong

Work with someone in your family to fill out this page.

I belong to the _____ family.

At Baptism I became a member of the Catholic Church.

I promise to pray for the whole Church; for my parish,

_____;

for my family; and for everyone who needs my prayers.

_____
(My Name)

_____
(Date)

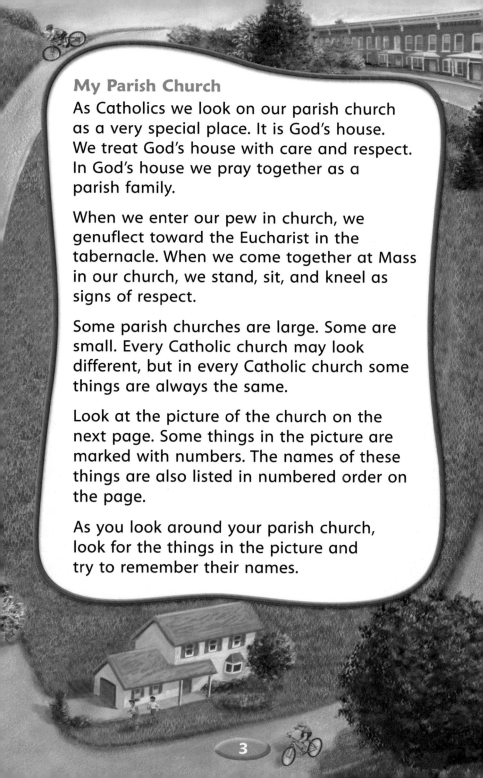

My Parish Church

As Catholics we look on our parish church as a very special place. It is God's house. We treat God's house with care and respect. In God's house we pray together as a parish family.

When we enter our pew in church, we genuflect toward the Eucharist in the tabernacle. When we come together at Mass in our church, we stand, sit, and kneel as signs of respect.

Some parish churches are large. Some are small. Every Catholic church may look different, but in every Catholic church some things are always the same.

Look at the picture of the church on the next page. Some things in the picture are marked with numbers. The names of these things are also listed in numbered order on the page.

As you look around your parish church, look for the things in the picture and try to remember their names.

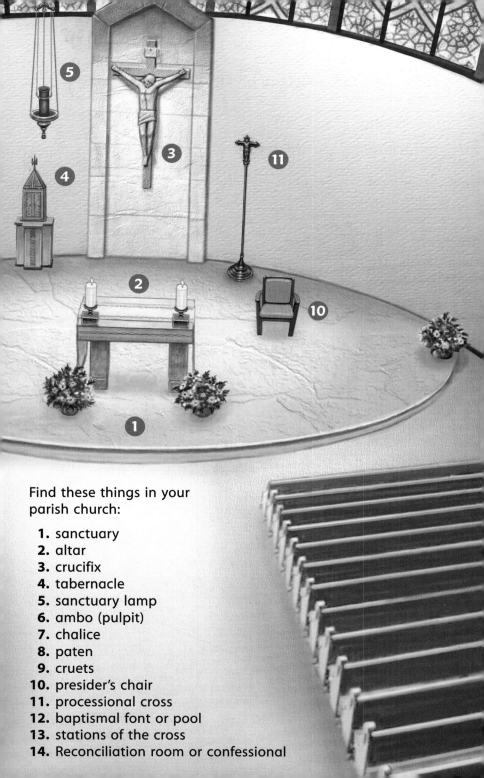

Find these things in your parish church:

1. sanctuary
2. altar
3. crucifix
4. tabernacle
5. sanctuary lamp
6. ambo (pulpit)
7. chalice
8. paten
9. cruets
10. presider's chair
11. processional cross
12. baptismal font or pool
13. stations of the cross
14. Reconciliation room or confessional

Introductory Rites

STAND

Entrance Song (Entrance Chant)
We sing to celebrate that we are gathered together with Jesus Christ and one another.

Greeting
We make the sign of the cross as the priest says:

☩ *In the name of the Father,*
and of the Son,
and of the Holy Spirit.

We respond: Amen.

The Mass

The priest welcomes everyone with these or other words:

> *The grace of our Lord Jesus Christ,*
> *and the love of God,*
> *and the communion of the Holy Spirit be*
> *with you all.*

We respond: And with your spirit.

God Forgives Us (Act of Penitence)
We ask God to forgive us.

Together we may pray:

> I confess to almighty God,
> and to you, my brothers and sisters,
> that I have greatly sinned,
> in my thoughts and in my words,
> in what I have done
> and in what I have failed to do,
> through my fault, through my fault,
> through my most grievous fault;
> therefore I ask blessed Mary ever-Virgin,
> all the Angels and Saints,
> and you, my brothers and sisters,
> to pray for me to the Lord our God.

We may repeat each line of the following prayer after the priest:

> Lord, have mercy.
> Christ, have mercy.
> Lord, have mercy.

Gloria

We praise God. We sing or say together:

Glory to God in the highest
and on earth peace to people of good will.

We praise you,
we bless you,
we adore you,
we glorify you,
we give you thanks for your great glory,
Lord God, heavenly King,
O God, almighty Father.

Lord Jesus Christ, Only Begotten Son,
Lord God, Lamb of God, Son of the Father,
you take away the sins of the world,
have mercy on us;
you take away the sins of the world,
receive our prayer;
you are seated at the right hand of the
Father,
have mercy on us.

For you alone are the Holy One,
you alone are the Lord,
you alone are the Most High,
Jesus Christ,
with the Holy Spirit,
in the glory of God the Father. Amen.

Opening Prayer (Collect)

The priest then says a short prayer.

We respond: Amen.

Liturgy of the Word

SIT

During this part of the Mass, we listen to God's Word from the Bible. The Bible readings tell us how much God loves and cares for us.

First Reading

We listen to a reading. This is usually from the Old Testament.

At the end of the reading, the lector, or reader, says:

> *The word of the Lord.*

We respond: Thanks be to God.

After the first reading, a psalm is read or sung. We say or sing a response.

Second Reading

We listen to a reading from the New Testament.

At the end of the reading, the lector says:

> *The word of the Lord.*

We respond: Thanks be to God.

STAND

Alleluia or Gospel Acclamation

As we stand for the reading of the gospel, we join in singing Alleluia. The Alleluia is a song of praise to God.

During Lent, instead of the Alleluia, we say other words of praise, such as:

> Praise to you, Lord Jesus Christ,
>   King of endless glory!

Gospel

In the gospel we hear the good news of Jesus.

Before proclaiming the gospel, the deacon or priest says:

> *The Lord be with you.*

We respond: And with your spirit.

The deacon or priest says:

> *A reading from the holy Gospel according to __ (Matthew, Mark, Luke, or John).*

We respond: Glory to you, O Lord.

At the end of the gospel, the deacon or priest says:

> *The Gospel of the Lord.*

We respond: Praise to you, Lord Jesus Christ.

Sit

Homily

We listen while the priest or deacon helps us to understand the Bible readings. We call this part of the Mass the homily.

Stand

Profession of Faith

In the Nicene Creed we say what we believe as members of the Catholic Church.

I believe in one God,
the Father almighty,
maker of heaven and earth,
of all things visible and invisible.

I believe in one Lord Jesus Christ,
the Only Begotten Son of God,
born of the Father before all ages.
God from God, Light from Light,
true God from true God,
begotten, not made, consubstantial with
the Father;
through him all things were made.
For us men and for our salvation
he came down from heaven,

and by the Holy Spirit
was incarnate of the Virgin Mary,
and became man.

For our sake he was crucified under
	Pontius Pilate,
	he suffered death and was buried,
	and rose again on the third day
		in accordance with the Scriptures.
	He ascended into heaven
		and is seated at the right hand of
			the Father.
He will come again in glory to judge the
	living and the dead
	and his kingdom will have no end.

I believe in the Holy Spirit, the Lord, the
	giver of life,
	who proceeds from the Father and
		the Son,
	who with the Father and the Son is
		adored and glorified,
	who has spoken through the prophets.
	I believe in one, holy, catholic and
		apostolic Church.
	I confess one Baptism for the
		forgiveness of sins
	and I look forward to the resurrection
		of the dead and the life of the world
			to come.
		Amen.

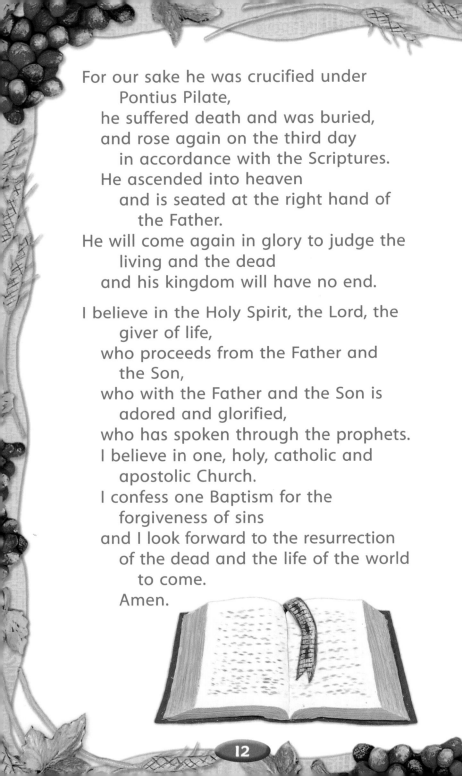

STAND

Prayer of the Faithful

During this prayer we pray for the Church and the leaders of the Church, for our country's leaders and world leaders, for all those in need, and for the salvation of the whole world.

After each prayer we respond with these or other words:

Lord, hear our prayer.

Liturgy of the Eucharist

SIT

The Preparation of the Gifts

As the Offertory chant, or song, is sung, our gifts of bread and wine are brought to the altar. Our gifts for the Church and the poor may also be brought forward.

The priest thanks God for the gift of bread.

We may pray: Blessed be God for ever.

Then the priest thanks God for the gift of wine.

We may pray: Blessed be God for ever.

The priest then prays that our gifts, our sacrifice, will be acceptable to God the Father.

STAND

We respond:

> May the Lord accept the sacrifice at your hands
> for the praise and glory of his name,
> for our good
> and the good of all his holy Church.

Prayer Over the Offerings

The priest asks God to accept our gifts.
> At the end of the prayer we say: Amen.

The Eucharistic Prayer

We join with the priest to give thanks and praise to God.

Preface

The priest begins by praying:

The Lord be with you.

We respond:

And with your spirit.

The priest prays:

Lift up your hearts.

We respond:

We lift them up to the Lord.

The priest prays:

Let us give thanks to the Lord our God.

We respond:

It is right and just.

At the end of the preface we all sing together.

Holy, Holy, Holy Lord God of hosts.
Heaven and earth are full of your glory.
   Hosanna in the highest.

Blessed is he who comes
       in the name of the Lord.
   Hosanna in the highest.

KNEEL

As the priest continues the Eucharistic Prayer, we remember what Jesus said and did at the Last Supper.

The priest takes the bread and says the words of Jesus:

TAKE THIS, ALL OF YOU, AND EAT OF IT,
FOR THIS IS MY BODY,
WHICH WILL BE GIVEN UP FOR YOU.

The priest holds up the consecrated bread, the Host, which is now the Body of Christ.

Then the priest takes the chalice, the cup of wine, and says the words of Jesus:

TAKE THIS, ALL OF YOU, AND DRINK FROM IT,
FOR THIS IS THE CHALICE OF MY BLOOD,
THE BLOOD OF THE NEW AND ETERNAL
COVENANT,
WHICH WILL BE POURED OUT FOR YOU AND FOR MANY
FOR THE FORGIVENESS OF SINS.
DO THIS IN MEMORY OF ME.

The priest holds up the chalice of consecrated wine that is now the Blood of Christ.

What looks and tastes like bread and wine is not bread and wine any more. By the power of the Holy Spirit and through the words and actions of the priest, the bread and wine have become the Body and Blood of Christ. Jesus Christ is really present in the Eucharist.

Then the priest asks us to proclaim our faith. We respond with these or other words:

We proclaim your Death, O Lord,
and profess your Resurrection
until you come again.

The priest and the people continue to pray. Then the priest raises the paten (a small, round plate) that holds the Body of Christ and the chalice that holds the Blood of Christ. The priest prays:

Through him, and with him, and in him,
O God, almighty Father, in the
unity of the Holy Spirit,
all glory and honor
is yours, for ever
and ever.

We respond: Amen.

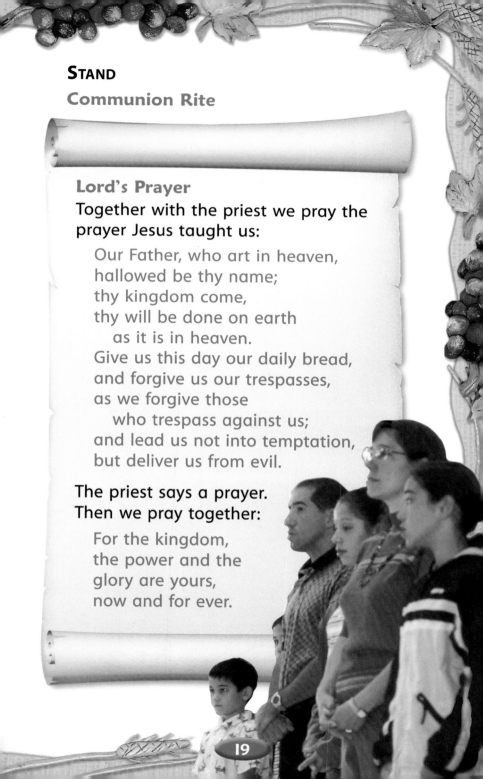

Communion Rite

Lord's Prayer

Together with the priest we pray the prayer Jesus taught us:

Our Father, who art in heaven,
hallowed be thy name;
thy kingdom come,
thy will be done on earth
   as it is in heaven.
Give us this day our daily bread,
and forgive us our trespasses,
as we forgive those
   who trespass against us;
and lead us not into temptation,
but deliver us from evil.

The priest says a prayer.
Then we pray together:

For the kingdom,
the power and the
glory are yours,
now and for ever.

Rite of Peace

The priest prays that Jesus Christ will give us the gift of peace.

We respond: Amen.

He then says:

The peace of the Lord be with you always.

We respond: And with your spirit.

We give a sign of peace to those around us.

STAND

Breaking of the Bread

We sing or say together this prayer for God's mercy and peace:

> Lamb of God, you take away the sins of
> the world,
> have mercy on us.
> Lamb of God, you take away the sins of
> the world,
> have mercy on us.
> Lamb of God, you take away the sins of
> the world,
> grant us peace.

As we pray the Lamb of God, the priest breaks the bread, called the Host, which has become the Body of Christ.

Holy Communion

Now we prepare to receive
Jesus Christ in Holy
Communion.

The priest says:

> *Behold the Lamb of God,
>   behold him who takes away
>   the sins of the world.
> Blessed are those called to
>   the supper of the Lamb.*

Together with the priest we pray:

> Lord, I am not worthy that you should
>   enter under my roof,
> but only say the word and my soul
>   shall be healed.

We sing a song as we come forward
to receive Holy Communion.

After we bow our head, the priest or
extraordinary minister of Holy
Communion places the Host in our
hand or on our tongue, saying:

> *The Body of Christ.*

We respond: Amen.

If we are receiving from the chalice, we bow our head again.

The priest or extraordinary minister of Holy Communion says:

The Blood of Christ.

We respond: Amen.

Then we take a sip from the chalice.

We return to our places and join in the Communion chant, or song.
We remember that Jesus is present within us.
We thank Jesus for the gift of himself in Holy Communion.

The priest invites us to pray and says a brief prayer.

We respond: Amen.

How I Receive Jesus in Holy Communion

When I receive the consecrated bread, or Host, this is what I do:

- ❖ I walk to the altar with hands joined.
- ❖ I think about Jesus, whom I will receive.
- ❖ As my turn comes, the priest or extraordinary minister raises the Host, and I bow my head.
- ❖ When I hear the words "the Body of Christ," I respond, "Amen."
- ❖ After the Host is placed in my hand or on my tongue, I step to the side. I swallow the Host and return to my seat.

If I am also going to receive from the chalice, I first swallow the Host. I move to the priest or extraordinary minister holding the chalice.

- ❖ The priest or extraordinary minister raises the chalice, and I bow my head.
- ❖ When I hear the words "the Blood of Christ," I respond, "Amen."
- ❖ Then I take a sip from the chalice.
- ❖ I return to my seat and sing the Communion chant, or song, with everyone.
- ❖ I spend time in quiet prayer.

Prayers Before Holy Communion

Before receiving the Body and Blood of Christ in Holy Communion, we should pause and think of what we are doing. We can say prayers like these:

My Lord and my God!

Jesus, you are the Bread of Life.
Thank you for sharing your life with me.
Help me always to be your friend and
disciple.

Prayers After Holy Communion

We remember that Jesus is with us. We can talk to him. We can tell him we love him. We can thank him. Here is a prayer you might also say:

Jesus, you do such great things for me!
You fill me with your life.
Help me to grow in loving you and
others.

Concluding Rites

STAND

At the end of the Mass, the priest asks God to bless everyone who is present.

Greeting

The priest prays:

The Lord be with you.

We respond: And with your spirit.

Blessing

The priest prays:

*May almighty God bless you, the Father, and the Son, †
and the Holy Spirit.*

We respond: Amen.

Dismissal

The priest or deacon then says:

Go and announce the Gospel of the Lord.

OR

Go forth, the Mass is ended.

OR

Go in peace, glorifying the Lord by your life.

OR

Go in peace.

We respond: Thanks be to God.

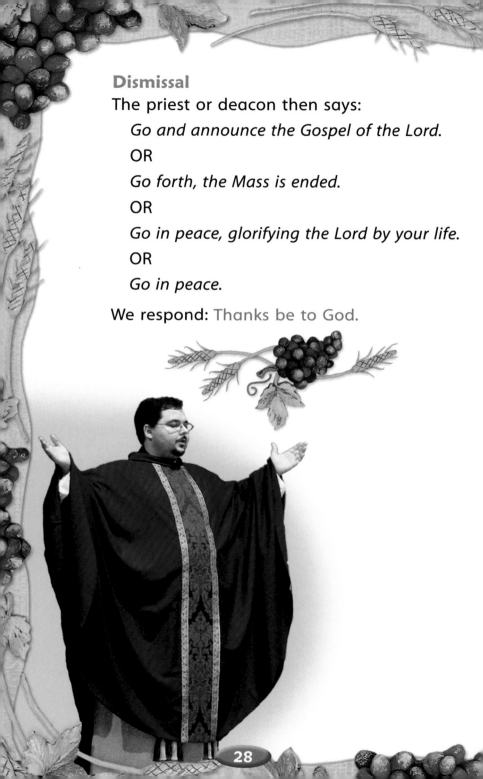

We Are Sent

We leave church praising God.

We go forth together to live as Jesus' disciples at home, at school, in our neighborhood, and in our parish.

Acknowledgments

Excerpts from the English translation of *The Roman Missal* **© 2010, International Committee on the Liturgy, Inc. All rights reserved.**

Excerpt from the *New American Bible with Revised New Testament and Psalms* Copyright © 1991, 1986, 1970 Confraternity of Christian Doctrine, Inc., Washington, DC. Used with permission. All rights reserved. No portion of the *New American Bible* may be reprinted without permission in writing from the copyright holder.

Excerpts from the English translation of *Rite of Penance* © 1974, ICEL; excerpt from the English translation of *A Book of Prayers* © 1982, ICEL. All rights reserved.

English translations of the Glory to the Father and Lord's Prayer by the International Consultation on English Texts (ICET).

"We Come to Ask Forgiveness" © 1986, Carey Landry and North American Liturgy Resources (NALR), 5536 NE Hassalo, Portland, OR 97213. All rights reserved. Used with permission. "Jesus, You Are Bread for Us" © 1988, Christopher Walker. Published by OCP Publications, 5536 NE Hassalo, Portland, OR 97213. All rights reserved. Used with permission.

Photo Credits
Mass Book
Jane Bernard: 19, 29; Karen Callaway: 6, 15, 16, 17, 18, 20, 21, 23, 27, 28; Crosiers/Gene Plaisted, OSC: 10, 22; W.P. Wittman Ltd.: 13.

Reconciliation and Prayer Book
Karen Callaway: 5, 6, 7, 8, 9, 10, 20, 34; Crosiers/Gene Plaisted, OSC: 12, 13; Neal Farris: 4, 17; Ken Karp: 16, 32; W.P. Wittman Ltd.: 24, 25.

Illustrator Credits
Mass Book
Laura Freeman: 24, 25, 26. Gary Phillips: 2, 3, 4, 5. Victoria Raymond: 6, 7, 8, 9, 10, 11, 12, 13, 14, 15, 16, 17, 18, 19, 20, 21, 22, 23, 24, 27, 28, 29.

Reconciliation and Prayer Book
Teresa Berasi: 2, 3, 4, 5, 6, 7, 8, 9, 10. Laura Freeman: 2, 4, 5, 11, 16, 17, 23, 26, 29, 31, 34, 35. Amanda Warren: 11, 12, 13, 14, 15, 16, 17, 20, 21, 22, 23, 24, 25, 26, 27, 28, 29, 30, 31, 32, 33.

Cover Illustrations
Teresa Berasi

My Reconciliation and Prayer Book

CONTENTS

Preparing for Penance and Reconciliation: How to Make Good and Loving Choices

1. When you have a choice to make, find a quiet place where you can think. Think about each of the choices, good and bad, that you can make.

2. Pray:
   Holy Spirit, help me to make good and loving choices.

3. Now think about each of your choices, and ask yourself these questions.

   Will this choice show that I love:
   ❖ God?
   ❖ others?
   ❖ myself?

   If I say "yes" to loving God, others, and myself, it is a good choice.

4. Ask someone you can trust to talk with you about your choices.

5. With God's help you can choose to do the good and loving thing.

The Sacrament of Penance and Reconciliation

Preparing for Penance and Reconciliation: The Ten Commandments

The Ten Commandments are God's special laws. Following the commandments helps us to live as God's children. We show our love for God, ourselves, and others by obeying the Ten Commandments.

1. I am the LORD your God: you shall not have strange gods before me.
2. You shall not take the name of the LORD your God in vain.
3. Remember to keep holy the LORD's Day.
4. Honor your father and your mother.
5. You shall not kill.
6. You shall not commit adultery.
7. You shall not steal.
8. You shall not bear false witness against your neighbor.
9. You shall not covet your neighbor's wife.
10. You shall not covet your neighbor's goods.

Preparing for Penance and Reconciliation: How to Examine Your Conscience

God has given each person a conscience. This gift helps a person to know what is right and what is wrong.

We can prepare to celebrate the sacrament of Penance and Reconciliation by examining our conscience. This means we think about our thoughts, words, and actions.

To examine your conscience, think quietly and prayerfully about the times you chose to do what you knew to be wrong. At these times you sinned, or disobeyed God's law on purpose.

To help you remember the times when you chose to do what you knew to be wrong, use questions like these. As you read each question, talk quietly to God about your answers.

❖ Have I prayed to God each day?

❖ Have I spoken God's name only with love and respect?

❖ Have I participated in Sunday Mass?

❖ Have I obeyed my parents and all those who care for me?

❖ Have I done anything to hurt myself or others?

❖ Have my actions shown love and respect for myself and others?

❖ Have I taken things that do not belong to me, or cheated in any way?

❖ Have I said mean things or told lies?

❖ Have I shown my feelings for other people in a loving and respectful way?

❖ Am I grateful for the things I have?

Celebrating the Sacrament of Penance and Reconciliation

The sacrament of Penance and Reconciliation can be celebrated individually with the priest or with the whole parish community and one or more priests.

These things are always part of the celebration of the sacrament of Penance and Reconciliation:

Contrition: I examine my conscience and am sorry for my sins. I promise not to sin again. During the sacrament I pray an act of contrition.

Confession: I tell my sins to a priest. The priest talks to me about loving God and others.

Penance: The priest tells me to say a prayer or do a kind act to show I am sorry for my sins. By doing my penance, I show I am willing to live as Jesus' disciple.

Absolution: The priest, acting in God's name, forgives my sins.

Celebrating Individually

First, I examine my conscience.

The priest greets me.

We both make the sign of the cross. The priest asks me to trust in God's mercy.

The priest or I may read from the Bible.

I talk with the priest and I confess my sins.

The priest talks to me about loving God and others. He gives me a penance.

I pray an act of contrition:

> My God,
> I am sorry for my sins with all my heart.
> In choosing to do wrong
> and failing to do good,
> I have sinned against you
> whom I should love above all things.
> I firmly intend, with your help,
> to do penance,
> to sin no more,
> and to avoid whatever leads
>   me to sin.
> Our Savior Jesus Christ
> suffered and died for us.
> In his name, my God,
> have mercy.

The priest extends his hand over my head and prays:

God, the Father of mercies,
through the death and resurrection
  of his Son
has reconciled the world to himself
and sent the Holy Spirit among us
for the forgiveness of sins;
through the ministry of the Church
may God give you pardon and peace,
and I absolve you from your sins
in the name of the Father, and
of the Son, †
and of the Holy Spirit.

I respond:

Amen.

Through these words and actions, I receive God's forgiveness of my sins.

Then the priest says:

Give thanks to the Lord, for he is good.

And I respond:

His mercy endures for ever.

The priest sends me out saying:

The Lord has freed you from your sins. Go in peace.

Celebrating with the Community

We sing an opening song.

The priest greets us.

The priest prays an opening prayer.

We listen to a reading from the Bible and a homily.

Each of us examines our conscience. Together, we pray an act of contrition.

We may say a prayer or sing a song. Then we pray the Our Father.

I meet individually with a priest to confess my sins. The priest gives me a penance. Then the priest gives me absolution.

After everyone has met individually with a priest, we thank God together for loving and forgiving us. The priest says a concluding prayer to thank God.

The priest blesses us. Then the priest dismisses us, saying, "The Lord has freed you from your sins. Go in peace."

We respond, "Thanks be to God."

Our Catholic Prayers and Practices

Prayer is talking and listening to God. We do this by using our own words or by saying prayers that we as Catholics pray.

We pray:
- ❖ to ask God for help
- ❖ to tell God how beautiful the world is
- ❖ to ask God to forgive us
- ❖ to pray for someone in need
- ❖ to thank God for his love
- ❖ to ask for God's blessing for us and others.

In the morning we can offer God all the things we will do that day. At night we can thank God for being with us all day.

God also wants us to pray as a parish community. We pray together when we gather for the celebration of Mass and the other sacraments.

From the beginning of the Church, the followers of Jesus have tried to live and act as Jesus taught. So they have passed on many of their prayers and practices.

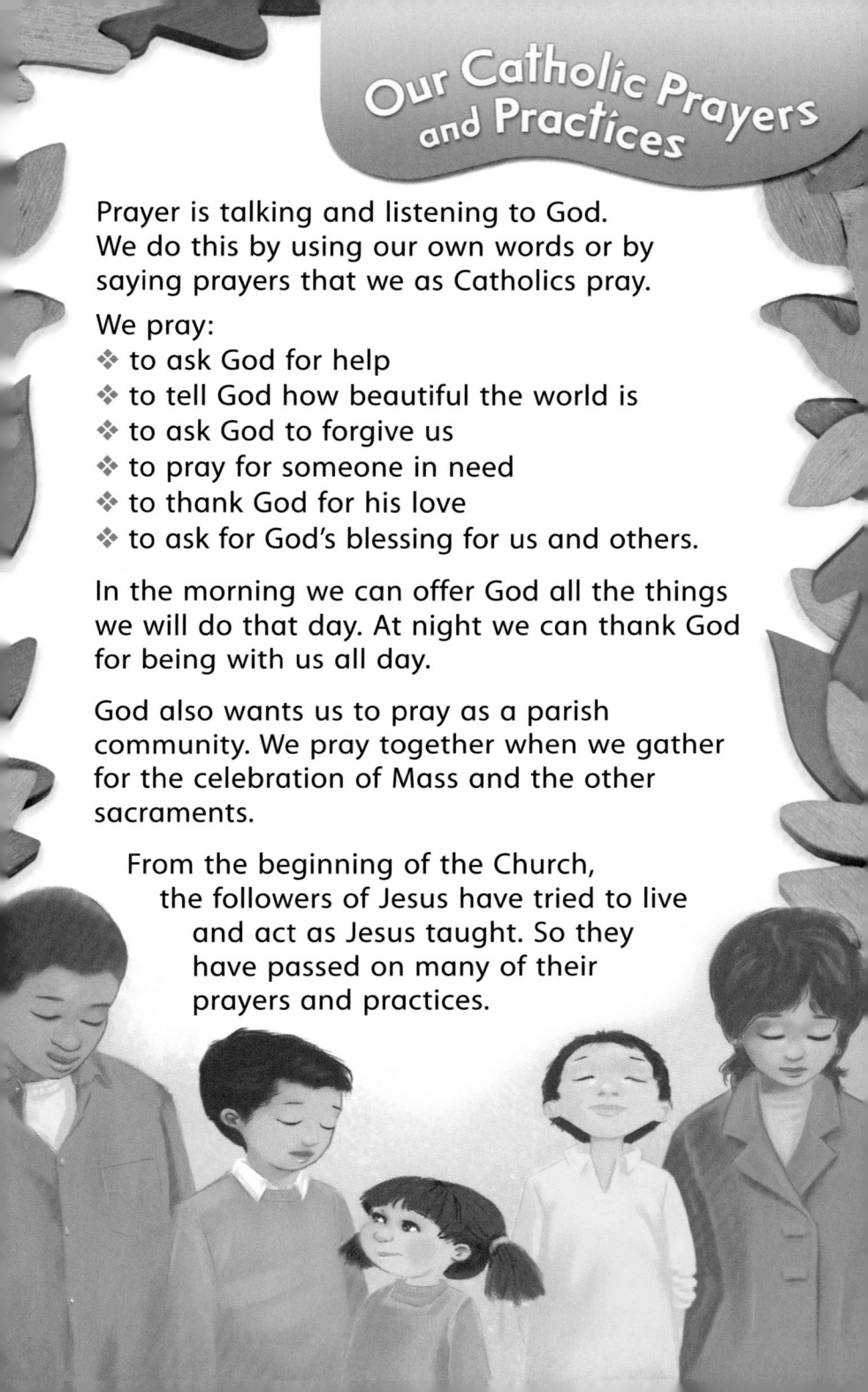

Sign of the Cross

In the name of the Father,
and of the Son,
and of the Holy Spirit. Amen.

Our Father

Our Father, who art in heaven,
hallowed be thy name:
thy kingdom come;
thy will be done on earth
as it is in heaven.
Give us this day our daily bread;
and forgive us our trespasses
as we forgive those
who trespass against us;
and lead us not into temptation,
but deliver us from evil. Amen.

Glory to the Father

Glory to the Father, and to the Son,
    and to the Holy Spirit:
as it was in the beginning,
    is now, and will be for ever. Amen.

Hail Mary

Hail Mary, full of grace,
the Lord is with you!
Blessed are you among women,
and blessed is the fruit
    of your womb, Jesus.
Holy Mary, Mother of God,
pray for us sinners,
now and at the hour of our death.
Amen.

The Apostles' Creed

I believe in God, the Father almighty,
    Creator of heaven and earth,
and in Jesus Christ, his only Son, our Lord,
who was conceived by the Holy Spirit,
born of the Virgin Mary,
suffered under Pontius Pilate,
    was crucified, died and was buried;
he descended into hell;
on the third day he rose again from the dead;
he ascended into heaven,
and is seated at the right hand
    of God the Father almighty;
from there he will come to judge
    the living and the dead.

I believe in the Holy Spirit,
    the holy catholic Church,
    the communion of saints,
    the forgiveness of sins,
    the resurrection of the body,
    and life everlasting. Amen.

The Angelus

The angel spoke God's message to Mary,
and she conceived of the Holy Spirit.
Hail Mary . . .

"I am the lowly servant of the Lord:
let it be done to me according to your word."
Hail Mary . . .

And the Word became flesh
and lived among us.
Hail Mary . . .

Pray for us, holy Mother of God,
that we may become worthy of the
    promises of Christ.

Let us pray.
Lord,
fill our hearts with your grace:
once, through the message of an angel
you revealed to us the Incarnation of your
    Son;
now, through his suffering and death
lead us to the glory of his resurrection.
We ask this through Christ our Lord.
Amen.

We begin our day asking for God's help to live as his friends.

Morning Offerings

1. My God, I offer you today
all that I think and do and say,
uniting it with what was done
on earth, by Jesus Christ, your Son.

2. My God, I offer you all my prayers,
works, and sufferings of this day
for all the intentions
of your most Sacred Heart. Amen.

We end our day giving thanks to God for his kindness and care.

An Evening Prayer

Dear God, before I sleep
I want to thank you for this day,
so full of your kindness and your joy.
I close my eyes to rest,
safe in your loving care.

These are prayers we can say before and after meals to thank God for all his gifts.

Grace Before Meals
Bless us, O Lord,
and these your gifts,
which we are about to receive
from your goodness,
through Christ our Lord.
Amen.

Grace After Meals
We give you thanks, almighty God,
for these and all your gifts,
which we have received
through Christ our Lord.
Amen.

Prayer for Someone Who Is Sick

Dear Jesus,
You touched and healed so many people
    when you were on earth.
Please, now, bring your healing love to

_____ (Name), who is sick.
Amen.

Prayer for Someone Who Has Died

Dear Jesus,
You told us that we will live forever
    in your love.

Take care of _____ (Name),
    and bring (him or her) to be with you
    in peace and joy.
Amen.

Prayer When I Need Help

Jesus,
You are my Good Shepherd.
Your love is all around me.
I know that you will love
    and care for me always.
Amen.

Prayer for Peace

Lord, make me an instrument of your peace:
where there is hatred, let me sow love;
where there is injury, pardon;
where there is doubt, faith;
where there is despair, hope;
where there is darkness, light;
where there is sadness, joy.

O divine Master, grant that I may not so
much seek
to be consoled as to console,
to be understood as to understand,
to be loved as to love.
For it is in giving that we receive,
it is in pardoning that we are
pardoned,
It is in dying that we are born
to eternal life.
Amen.

Saint Francis of Assisi

Visits to the Most Blessed Sacrament

At Mass, after Holy Communion, there may be consecrated Hosts that have not been received. These Hosts are placed in the tabernacle and are called the Most Blessed Sacrament. The Most Blessed Sacrament is another name for the Eucharist.

Often, people visit the church and pray to Jesus, who is present in the Most Blessed Sacrament. We call this practice "making a visit" to the Most Blessed Sacrament.

We can tell Jesus of our love for him and thank him. We can tell him about our needs and our hopes. We can ask Jesus to help us love and care for others.

Prayer Before the Most Blessed Sacrament

Jesus,
you are God-with-us,
especially in this sacrament of the Eucharist.
You love me as I am
and help me grow.

Come and be with me
in all my joys and sorrows.
Help me share your peace and love
with everyone I meet.
I ask in your name.
Amen.

Benediction

At Benediction the Most Blessed Sacrament is placed in a special holder called a monstrance. As we look at the monstrance, we remember that Jesus is really present in the Eucharist.

During Benediction the priest lifts the monstrance and blesses the people. Everyone makes the sign of the cross and bows in reverence before the Most Blessed Sacrament.

The Rosary

The rosary is a prayer in honor of Mary. We pray the rosary using a special set of beads. We begin by praying the Sign of the Cross. Then we hold the cross, or crucifix, and pray the Apostles' Creed.

On the first large bead we pray the Our Father. On each of the three smaller beads that follow, we pray a Hail Mary. After these prayers we pray one Glory to the Father.

For each decade we pray an Our Father on the large bead and a Hail Mary on each of the ten smaller beads. At the end of each decade, we pray the Glory to the Father. We end the rosary with a special prayer to Mary called the Hail, Holy Queen.

While we are praying the rosary, we think of events in the lives of Jesus and Mary. We call these events the mysteries of the rosary.

The Five Joyful Mysteries
1. The Annunciation
2. The Visitation
3. The Birth of Jesus
4. The Presentation of Jesus in the Temple
5. The Finding of Jesus in the Temple

The Five Sorrowful Mysteries
1. The Agony in the Garden
2. The Scourging at the Pillar
3. The Crowning with Thorns
4. The Carrying of the Cross
5. The Crucifixion and Death of Jesus

The Five Glorious Mysteries
1. The Resurrection
2. The Ascension
3. The Descent of the Holy Spirit upon the Apostles
4. The Assumption of Mary into Heaven
5. The Coronation of Mary as Queen of Heaven

The Five Mysteries of Light
1. Jesus' Baptism in the Jordan
2. The Miracle at the Wedding at Cana
3. Jesus Announces the Kingdom of God
4. The Transfiguration
5. The Institution of the Eucharist

The Stations of the Cross

In many parishes there are special pictures or sculptures around the church called Stations of the Cross. There are fourteen stations, or places to stop. At each station we think and pray about what is happening to Jesus. This reminds us how much Jesus loves us and that he suffered and died for us. We often pray the stations during Lent.

Here is a prayer that you can pray at each station:

> Thank you, Jesus,
> for all you have done for us.
> We know that through
> your cross and Resurrection
> you have saved the world.

The Stations of the Cross

1. Jesus is condemned to die.
2. Jesus takes up his cross.
3. Jesus falls the first time.
4. Jesus meets his mother.
5. Simon helps Jesus carry his cross.
6. Veronica wipes the face of Jesus.
7. Jesus falls the second time.
8. Jesus meets the women of Jerusalem.
9. Jesus falls the third time.
10. Jesus is stripped of his garments.
11. Jesus is nailed to the cross.
12. Jesus dies on the cross.
13. Jesus is taken down from the cross.
14. Jesus is laid in the tomb.

Sacramentals

As Catholics we use sacramentals to remind us of Jesus, Mary, and the saints. We use them to help us think about God's love.

Sacramentals are blessings, actions, and special objects given to us by the Church. We show respect for these special things we use in the celebration of our faith. Sacramentals include blessed oil, holy water, palms, ashes, and candles. Sacramentals also include blessed medals, rosaries, statues, and paintings.

Actions are sacramentals, too. We make the sign of the cross with holy water. This reminds us of our Baptism. We also make the sign of the cross as the priest blesses us during Mass and the sacraments.

Each year on the feast of Saint Blaise, all those who wish to pray for good health can attend the blessing of throats. Blessings are the most important sacramentals.

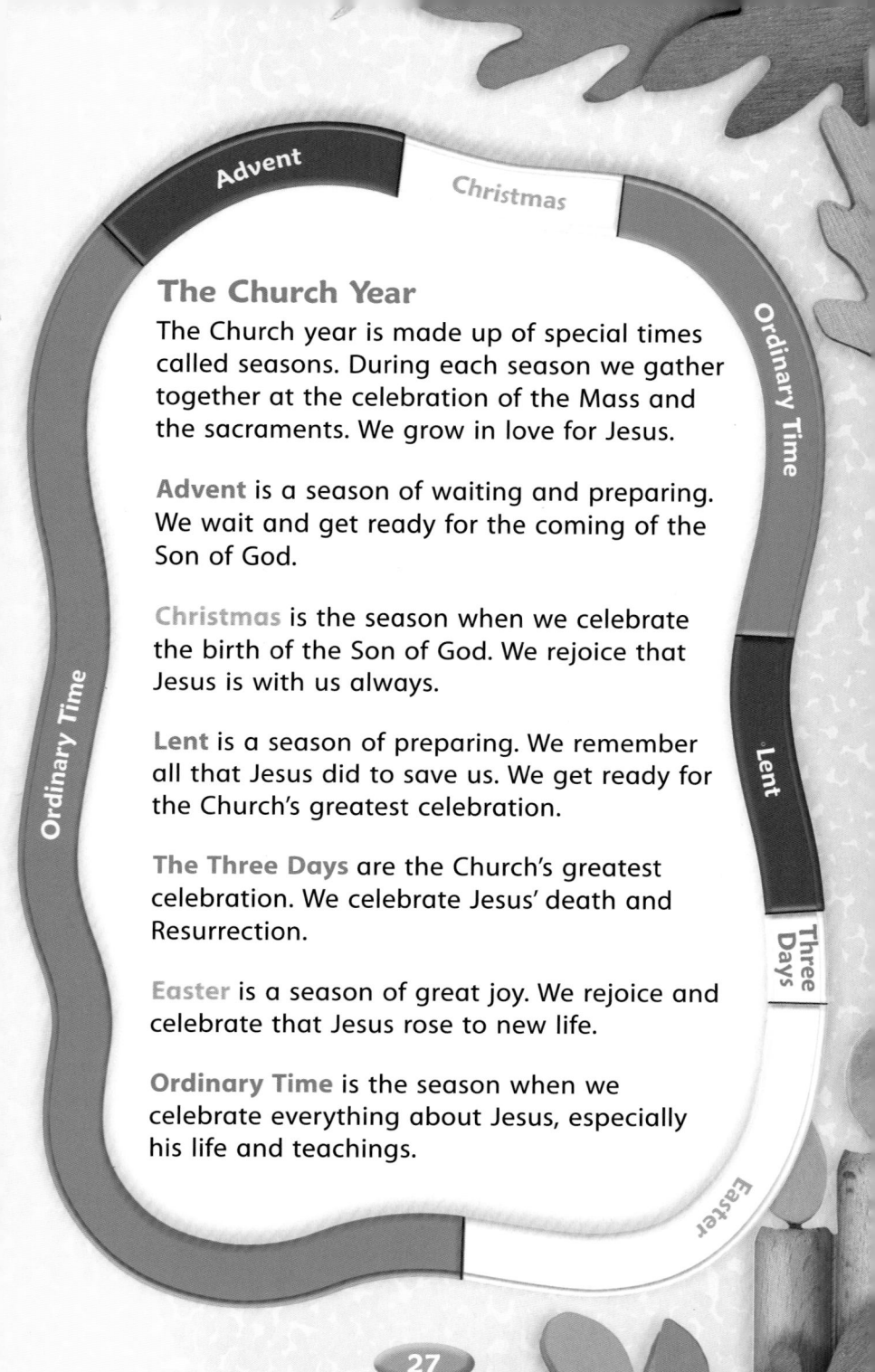

The Church Year

The Church year is made up of special times called seasons. During each season we gather together at the celebration of the Mass and the sacraments. We grow in love for Jesus.

Advent is a season of waiting and preparing. We wait and get ready for the coming of the Son of God.

Christmas is the season when we celebrate the birth of the Son of God. We rejoice that Jesus is with us always.

Lent is a season of preparing. We remember all that Jesus did to save us. We get ready for the Church's greatest celebration.

The Three Days are the Church's greatest celebration. We celebrate Jesus' death and Resurrection.

Easter is a season of great joy. We rejoice and celebrate that Jesus rose to new life.

Ordinary Time is the season when we celebrate everything about Jesus, especially his life and teachings.

Advent

Christmas

Ordinary Time

Lent

Three Days

Easter

Ordinary Time

Celebrating the Season of Advent

The Church year begins with the four weeks of Advent. During Advent we prepare to celebrate the coming of Jesus Christ. We celebrate at home and in our parish.

One way to celebrate this season is to gather around an Advent wreath. This wreath is made of evergreen branches and has four candles. There is one candle for each week of Advent. We light the candles to remind us to watch and wait for the coming of the Son of God. We pray: Come, Lord Jesus!

Celebrating the Christmas Season

During the Christmas season we celebrate God's greatest gift to us, his Son, Jesus. We remember that Jesus is the Light of the World. He is with us now and forever.

The season starts on Christmas Eve and ends on the feast of the Baptism of the Lord.

During the Christmas season we also celebrate the feast days of the Holy Family, the Epiphany, and Mary, the Mother of God.

Celebrating the Season of Lent

Lent is the time of preparation before Easter. During the forty days of Lent we remember all that Jesus did to save us.

Lent begins on a day called Ash Wednesday. On this day Catholics are marked with blessed ashes. The ashes are used to mark a cross on our foreheads.

The cross of ashes reminds us that Jesus suffered and died for us. It is a sign that we are sorry for our sins and want to follow Jesus. During Lent we pray, do good things for others, and help people who are poor.

The last week of Lent is called Holy Week. It begins on Passion Sunday, also called Palm Sunday. We remember that just days before his passion and death, Jesus went to Jerusalem and was greeted by the people with great joy. They waved palm branches in the air, shouting: "Hosanna to the Son of David" (Matthew 21:9).

On this day palms are blessed and given out. They remind us that we should always welcome and honor Jesus, who died for us.

Celebrating the Three Days

The Three Days are the most important days of the Church year. We gather with our parish to celebrate. The celebration of the Three Days begins on Holy Thursday evening and ends on Easter Sunday evening.

On Holy Thursday we remember what happened at the Last Supper. We celebrate that Jesus gave himself to us in the Eucharist. We remember the ways Jesus served others.

On Good Friday we listen to the story of Jesus' death. We pray before the cross. The cross reminds us of Jesus' dying and rising to new life.

On Holy Saturday night we light the Easter candle to show that Jesus has risen. This reminds us that Jesus is the Light of the World. We listen to Bible readings about the great things God has done for us. We celebrate that Jesus rose from the dead.

On Holy Saturday we remember our Baptism in a special way. We also welcome new members of the Church as they are baptized.

Celebrating the Easter Season

As Holy Saturday turns into Easter Sunday, we begin the Easter season. We celebrate the Eucharist and rejoice that Christ is risen.

The Easter season lasts for fifty days. It ends on Pentecost Sunday. During the Easter season we give thanks for the new life Jesus brings us.

On Pentecost Sunday we remember the day when the Holy Spirit came upon the apostles.

Celebrating in Ordinary Time

We celebrate the season of Ordinary Time twice each year. Ordinary Time comes between the seasons of Christmas and Lent. Ordinary Time comes again between the seasons of Easter and Advent.

In Ordinary Time we celebrate Jesus and everything about him. We learn how to follow Jesus in our everyday lives and how to grow closer to him each day.

Praying at Home with My Family

We can pray to God at any time and in any place. We can pray when we are alone, and we can pray with others.

When we are at home we can pray with our family. Some families pray together before and after meals. Other families pray together at bedtime. Many families pray the rosary together.

Some families set aside a special prayer space. A prayer space is a place to pray, either together or alone.

In the prayer space you might have a table. The table can hold a cross, a Bible, or a book of favorite prayers.

In the prayer space you might also have pictures or statues of Jesus, Mary, and your favorite saints. You can decorate your family prayer space for each season of the Church year.

My Family Prays Together

My family's favorite prayers:

_____

_____

_____

_____

My family's favorite feasts and practices:

_____

_____

_____

_____

My family's favorite saints:

_____

_____

_____

_____

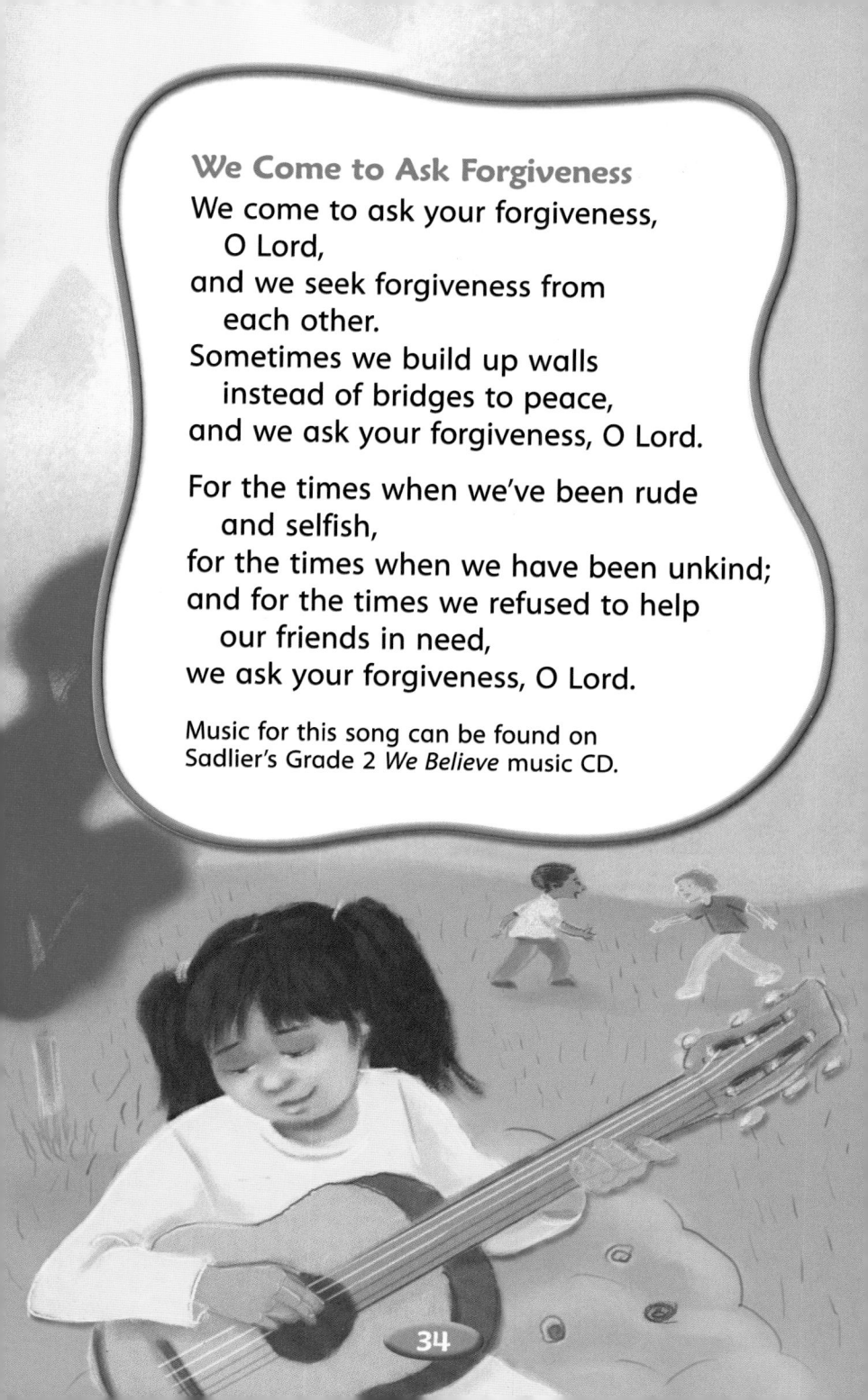

We Come to Ask Forgiveness

We come to ask your forgiveness,
   O Lord,
and we seek forgiveness from
   each other.
Sometimes we build up walls
   instead of bridges to peace,
and we ask your forgiveness, O Lord.

For the times when we've been rude
   and selfish,
for the times when we have been unkind;
and for the times we refused to help
   our friends in need,
we ask your forgiveness, O Lord.

Music for this song can be found on
Sadlier's Grade 2 *We Believe* music CD.

Songs

Jesus, You Are Bread for Us

Jesus, you are bread for us.
Jesus, you are life for us.
In your gift of Eucharist
we find love.

When we feel we need a friend,
you are there with us, Jesus.
Thank you for the friend you are.
Thank you for the love we share.

Music for this song can be found on
Sadlier's Grade 2 *We Believe* music CD.